9/00

W9-BHG-536

MIDLOTHIAN
PUBLIC LIBRARY

DATE DUE

CHICKENS

A TRUE BOOK

by

Sara Swan Miller

Children's Press®
A Division of Grolier Publishing

New York London Hong Kong Sydney
Danbury, Connecticut

Brown and white eggs

Content Consultant
Jan Jenner, Ph.D.

Reading Consultant
Linda Cornwell
Coordinator of School Quality
and Professional Improvement
Indiana State Teachers
Association

Author's Dedication
For Jane and the "chickens"

Visit Children's Press® on
the Internet at:
http://publishing.grolier.com

Library of Congress Cataloging-in-Publication Data

Miller, Sara Swan
    Chickens / by Sara Swan Miller.
        p.   cm. — (A True book)
    Includes bibliographical references and index.
    Summary: Describes the physical traits, lifestyle, and behavior of chick-
ens and their role in providing humans with meat.
    ISBN 0-516-21576-0 (lib. bdg.)   ISBN 0-516-27180-6 (pbk.)
    1. Chickens Juvenile literature. [1. Chickens.] I. Title. II. Series.
SF487. 5. M55   2000
636. 5—dc21   99-30130

GROLIER
PUBLISHING

Contents

Chickens are friendly and easy to raise.

The Chicken Story

You know where eggs come from, of course—chickens! But do you know what chickens are like? Do you know what it's like to raise them?

The eggs and chickens you buy at the store come mostly from huge factory farms. But many people still

Eggs are a popular meal, any time of the day.

keep chickens on small farms. A lot of people even raise them in their backyards. Why? Isn't it easier just to buy packaged chicken or eggs in the store? If you have ever eaten eggs or chickens raised on a small farm, you know they taste much better!

Of all the food animals, chickens are the most popular. There are six chickens for every human in the world. People first tamed wild chickens more than five thousand years ago in Asia. It wasn't very hard because chickens like to stay in one place. All people needed to do was

These chickens flock together in the open air.

give them a nice place to stay and some food.

The first chickens were thin and small. They didn't lay many eggs. Over the years, people improved them. They kept choosing the best birds

Chicks in a chicken hatchery

to mate with each other. That made better and better chicks.

Now there are many different breeds, or kinds of chickens. Some breeds lay more eggs. Others give more meat. Some breeds are raised mostly for

shows because they are so pretty. There are more than fifty breeds in the United States alone. And there are many different types of each breed. That's a lot of different kinds of chickens to choose from!

Chicken Names

When a chicken first hatches out of its shell, it is called a chick.

When it gets a little older, it is called a chicken.

A Barred Rock rooster

A grown female is called a hen.

A Barred Rock hen

A grown male is called a rooster.

Some Favorite Breeds

Leghorns are slim chickens that lay a lot of big eggs. These are the chickens that lay the white eggs people buy in stores.

Hubbards are white, heavy chickens that people raise for their meat.

The eggs you see in stores begin the journey here.

A Rhode Island Red chicken (left) and a Red Jungle Fowl (right)

Many people on small farms raise Rhode Island Reds. These chickens are friendly. They are fun to have around.

Bantams are only half as big as regular chickens. People love to have them on their farms because they are so charming.

14

White Crested Black Polish
chickens are very odd-looking.
They have such long feathers
on their heads that you can
hardly see their eyes and beaks.
People raise them mostly to
put in shows.

A fancy breed of
black rooster

What Are Chickens Like?

Chickens are always pecking and scratching. They peck here and peck there, eating a little at a time. Sometimes they stop to rub their beaks on the ground. That's how they keep them sharp.

This chicken is busy pecking and scratching for bits of food.

Thirsty chickens crowd around a waterer.

Inside a pen chickens eat chicken feed people give them. They drink out of special waterers. You might see a chicken dip its beak in the water. Then it holds its head back. The water trickles down its throat.

Some people let their chickens out of their pen. Then the
chickens busily hunt for seeds,
small plants, fruits, berries,
insects, and worms.

Chickens leave
the coop to search
for tasty morsels
in the hay.

When a chicken eats, the food goes into an organ called the gizzard. The gizzard looks like a small bag. There are little pebbles inside the gizzard that the chicken has also eaten. The pebbles grind the food inside the gizzard. Then the food goes down into the chicken's stomach.

Newly hatched chicks learn about what is good to eat by pecking. They peck at shiny things because they look like

Baby chicks stay close to the mother hen as they peck for food.

water. Sometimes they even peck at their own toes.

When they are not pecking for food, chickens run their feathers through their beaks

There's plenty of dust here for this chicken to use.

to clean them. This is called preening. They also like a good dust bath every day. The dust helps get rid of annoying insects on a chicken's skin.

All Kinds of Combs

Chickens have red combs on their heads and red wattles under their chins. The wattle is the fleshy skin that hangs under a chicken's beak. A rooster's comb is bigger and brighter than a hen's comb. Different breeds have different shaped combs.

A Barred Rock rooster

A Maran hen

Look closely for this rooster's spurs at the back of its legs.

Roosters have spurs on the back of their legs. Sometimes they use them to fight with each other or to drive off enemies. Roosters crow early

"Rooster fight!"

in the morning and often during the day. They may be saying, "Look! Food!" or "Watch out! Hawk!" or maybe just, "Here I am!"

A fancy breed of rooster and hen, known for frizzled, or curly, feathers

Hens can lay eggs without a rooster. But for chicks to hatch from them, the hens need to mate with a rooster. That makes the eggs fertile. Some breeds lay white eggs. Some lay brown eggs. There are even chickens that lay blue or green eggs.

A farmer with three good laying hens will get about two eggs a day. Each hen lays about twenty dozen eggs in her first year. After that, it lays fewer each year. In winter, when days are short, hens stop laying eggs until spring.

Chickens like to be together in small flocks. They all know their place because they have

This flock of hens is called free range because they roam the land freely.

a social order called a pecking order. One chicken is the leader of the flock. It pecks the others to let them know it is boss. The rest of the chick-ens may be the boss of other chickens. At the bottom of the pecking order is one chicken that is bossed by all the rest.

All chickens know their place in the pecking order. The pecking order helps keep them from fighting over food. They know who gets first choice.

These chickens, called broilers, feed in a certain order.

It's important to be calm around chickens. They get scared easily. They flutter about and call "Brrr!" That's why a timid person is called a chicken!

Chickens can be a lot of fun. Once they get to know you, they will come when you call them. They will let you pick them up and pet them. They will eat out of your hand, too. They might even sit on your shoulder when

you walk around the yard.
That is another reason people
like keeping chickens.

Chickens on a Small Farm

Most chickens today are raised on factory farms. Factory farms are not chickens' natural environment. They live crowded together in small cages. The cages are stacked on top of each other in huge barns. There may be more than

This factory farm lets in sunlight, while others do not.

100,000 chickens in one barn! These chickens never get to run around or bask in the sunlight.

This may be why their meat and eggs are less tasty than the meat and eggs of home-raised chickens.

On a small farm, chickens can spend their days pecking and scratching about in a fenced-in yard. When it is too hot or too wet, they can go into their chicken coop. At night, they all go into the coop to roost.

Chickens can't see well at night. There are raccoons, weasels, foxes, and other animals outside that want to eat them. The farmer locks the door of the chicken coop at

A red fox in search of a chicken dinner

night to keep the chickens safe. But the rest of the time they can go and come as they like.

The farmer gives them chicken feed in a special feeder. It is built so the chickens do not scatter the feed on the ground and waste it.

A chicken always needs fresh water. It can only drink a little at a time, so it drinks often. In the winter, the farmer brings the chickens warm water several times a day.

Feed often has vitamins and minerals added to keep chickens healthy.

The farmer also gives the chickens small pebbles called grit to help them grind their food in their gizzards. They need extra calcium, a mineral that makes their eggs strong. People need calcium, too, to build strong bones.

Sometimes the farmer gives the chickens special treats. They love cracked corn and a

This chicken enjoys an apple with friends.

grain mixture called scratch. They like leftovers, too. Lettuce, apple and carrot peels, tomatoes, and bits of toast are always welcome!

Inside the coop the chickens have a perch to roost on at night. It may be a tree branch, a fence post, or an old ladder. They also have nest boxes to lay their eggs in. The farmer lines them with straw or sawdust to keep the eggs clean.

For safety, chickens like to perch high above the ground at night.

Twice a day the farmer collects the eggs. If there are too many to use, they may sell them to their neighbors. Others they may keep to hatch into chicks.

Chickens raised on a small farm seem much more contented than factory farm chickens. They get to roam about, pecking for food and taking dust baths whenever they want. In the crowded cages in factory farms, chickens try to peck each other. But on a farm, chickens cluck quietly and even sing a little song. It sounds like a soft, chuckled, "Burrt, burrt, burrt."

Chickens in a barnyard feast on pumpkin.

To Find Out More

Here are some additional resources to help you learn more about chickens:

 **Books**

Brady, Peter. **Chickens.**
Bridgestone Books, 1996.

Jeunesse, Gallimard. **Farm Animals.** Scholastic, 1998.

Johnson, Sylvia and Kiyoshi Shimizu. **Inside an Egg.** Lerner Publications, 1987.

Radtke, Becky. **Farm Activity Book.** Dover Publications, 1997.

Saunders-Smith, Gail. **Chickens.** Pebble Books, 1997.

Selsam, Millicent. **From Egg to Chick.** Harpercrest, 1987.

Webster, Charlie. **Farm Animals.** Barron's, 1997.

Organizations and Online Sites

Chicken Cam
http://www.snuggeybug. com/

This site has pictures of a few different breeds of chickens, including some sent in by people who raise their own chickens.

Feathersite
http://www.cyborganic.com /people/feathersite/Poultry /BRKPoultryPage.html

If you want to see pictures of many different breeds of poultry, including baby chicks, this is an excellent site. It also gives some information about raising chickens.

Information Dirt Road: The 4-H Farm at the University of California, Irvine
http://www.ics.uci.edu/ ~pazzani/4H/InfoDirt.html

This site contains information on raising different kinds of farm animals, including chickens.

Kids Farm
www.kidsfarm.com

Kids Farm is a lot of fun and educational, too. It is created by people who run a farm in the Colorado Rocky Mountains and brings you real sights and sounds of animals on the farm.

Important Words

comb the fleshy crest on top of a chicken's head

coop a small building for housing chickens

dozen group of twelve

factory farm a large farm where thousands of chickens are raised for meat and eggs

gizzard an organ inside a chicken where its food is ground with pebbles

pecking order the way chickens organize themselves from the most important to the least important

preening cleaning feathers with the beak

scratch a grain mixture fed to chickens

wattle the fleshy skin that hangs under a chicken's beak

Index

Meet the Author

Sara Swan Miller has enjoyed working with children all her life, first as a nursery-school teacher, and later as an outdoor environmental educator at the Mohonk Preserve in New Paltz, New York. Now Ms. Miller is a full-time writer. She has written more than thirty books for children, including *Cows, Goats, Pigs*, and *Sheep*, in the True Books series.

Photographs ©: David R. Frazier: 21, 34, 38; Midwestock: 15 (Jim Hays); Norvia Behling: 11 left, 11 bottom right, 26, 31; Photo Researchers: 36 (Alan D. Carey), 25 (Gregory K. Scott); PhotoEdit: 6 (D. Young-Wolff); Superstock, Inc.: 4, 13, 39; Tony Stone Images: cover (Birgid Allig), 23 left (Peter Cade), 28 (Peter Dean), 8 (Tony Page), 23 right (Kevin Schafer), 1 (Trevor Wood); Visuals Unlimited: 43 (Kevin & Betty Collins), 2 (A. J. Copley), 17, 22 (John D. Cunningham), 10 (Derrick Ditchburn), 9 (Jeff Greenberg), 19 (Valorie Hodgson), 41 (John Sohlden), 18, 29 (Inga Spence), 24 (Betsy R. Strasser), 33 (S. Strickland/Naturescapes), 14 right (Milton H. Tierney, Jr.), 11 top right (Ken Wagner), 14 left (William J. Weber).